There Is Hope

Poems From The Heart For The Heart

by
Debby Paine

*For Grandma + Grandpa
from Hal and Becky
with Love.*

There Is Hope
Poems From the Heart, For the Heart

Copyright 1998 © by Debby Paine
All Rights Reserved. No Portion of this Book may be reproduced, stored in a retrieval system, or transmitted in any form or by any means - electronic, mechanical, photocopy, recording - or any other - except for brief quotations in printed reviews, without prior permission of the author.

Cover and Photograph © 1998 Hal Noss

Library of Congress, Register of Copyrights
Washington, D.C.

ISBN 0-9668961-0-6

Scripture taken from the Holy Bible
New International Version
Copyright 1973, 1978, 1984 International Bible Society
Used by permission of Zondervan Bible Publishers

Golden Quill Press
159 Route 304
Bardonia, NY 10954

There is Hope
Contents

There is Hope for the Struggling

Hope	1
Your Garden of Hope	2
I Wish	3
When God Remains Silent	4
Blame	5
Are You?	6
Jesus's Tears	7
Lord, Help!	8
Lies	9
Handles	10
Bitterness	11
How Dare You?	12
Shame	13
Castaways	14
Trust	15
Shepherd	16
Mercy	17
Sunday's Best	18
Church Greetings	20
Hold on to Hope	21

There is Hope for the Hurting

Tears	23
God's Lap	24
Come, Cry With Me	25
For Kyle	27
Forgiven	28
Betrayal	29
The Gift of Regret	30
Wall of Pain	31
My Church	33
For Now	36

There is Hope for the Caring

Forgiveness	38
Lord, Let Me Be...	39
A Rainbow of Love	40
Dear Birth Mom	41
To Be	42
Be Like Mom	43
My Grandma's Hands	44
This Jar of Clay	46
A Friend Just Like You	47
Shadow	48
The Gift I Call "You"	49

There is Hope for the Searching

My Most Common Prayer	51
From Memories to Dreams	52
A Priceless Treasure	53
Like a Child	54
So I Can Praise You	55
I've Been Held in His Arms	56
Forever Friends	57
Heaven	58
Remember	59
The Cup and the Bread	61
Home	62

"May the God of HOPE fill you with all joy and peace as you trust in Him, so that you may overflow with HOPE by the power of the Holy Spirit."
Romans 15:13

*This collection is dedicated to my Dad and Mom —
John and Ethel Cobaugh.
I love you.*

Dad and Mom, you understand, more than most people what the Apostle Paul meant when he wrote to the people of Rome:

"...And we rejoice in the HOPE of the glory of God. Not only so, but we also rejoice in our sufferings, because we know that suffering produces perseverence; perseverence, character; and character, HOPE. And HOPE does not disappoint us, because God has poured out His love into our hearts by the Holy Spirit, whom he has given us."
Romans 5:2 - 5

Acknowledgments

To thank everyone who contributed to this book would mean thanking every person who has ever passed through my life - even for a moment, for I have learned from them or with them. But there are many who deserve special thanks... my co-workers and friends at The Tanning Zone, my special "Church family," who have trusted - and encouraged my writing through these years. To each one who has asked me to write a poem for their special situation and allowed me to share it so others can benefit from their open, revealing hearts - a Special "Thank You."

Francine Cefola and Bobbi Murbi, my new friends at Golden Quill Press, have made the most wonderful suggestions. I appreciate your help, encouragement and patience - so much. I will never take any book for granted again. Thank you!

Paula Sabul, who doesn't understand what a precious instrument of God she is to so many people - but, especially to me. I love you, and thank God for you.

Helen and John Ellenberger who have held on to me, believed in me, and walked with me through my life's hardest moments. You are a blessing in so many lives, but none more than mine. I cherish you both.

Coetta and Armand Rappaport who share their hearts and visions and incredible encouragement, Big Hugs, Lots of Love and Thank You's.

Lorna, my cousin and Aunt Flo, who never give up on me... I love you...

Dan, my brother, Gloria and Kim, my sisters, and each of their families who give and give and give some more... Thank you's will never do. To all of the "Paines" in my life - God Bless you! I have learned so much from you! And, I have the greatest nephews and nieces in the world because of all of you.

Tammy, this hug's for you...

I have always said, "God gave us wonderful children," and He has! Becky, Bobby, and Michael have taught me more about compassion, forgiveness and love than could be written in a thousand books; and now, the loves in their lives - Hal, Amy and Iris have made our lives even richer.

And to my husband, Phil, who makes all my dreams come true - the best dream of all is you - loving me! All the words in the world could never say how special you've made that dream.

There Is Hope...

Dear Reader,

Maybe it doesn't feel like it right now...

Maybe you're struggling with an unhappy marriage, a battle-filled divorce, rebellious children, an illness, or even the death of someone you love.

Maybe you're dealing with the loss of a job, a home, a friendship, or your faith in God.

Maybe you've lost someone you love. Maybe you've given up custody, or placed a child up for adoption.

Maybe you're contending with yourself – with a sense of failure, of shame, of an inability to overcome some habit, a secret that no one knows about, a lie that you don't want to live anymore.

Maybe you think there is just no hope - for you - for your situation - for your life. But, my friend, there is.

I tried to find a word for "no hope" in the dictionary. I couldn't find one! "Hopeless" means that – less hope... Even "hope against hope" is defined as 'hoping in vain'... The opposite of hope is defeat, doubt, giving up... That doesn't mean there is NO hope - it simply means that one has stopped hoping.

This collection of poems is about life - about people going through all kinds of experiences, but always held together by a common thread - HOPE.

You may wonder why some of the poems are included... In the last few years, I have been asked to write poems for people going through every kind of pain; and in the process, have learned that there is no one whose situation is totally unique to them. There is comfort in knowing that we are not alone in our struggles, our fears, our doubts, our trials. Knowing that can give us hope!

This collection of poems is not about believing what I believe, or of knowing God the way I do. It is about reaching toward that thread of hope when it is all that you have the strength to do. I know. I have been there.

I do not know you or your situation, but I "HOPE" this book will fall open to the page with the words that you need for your heart today. Cry if you need to, forgive if you should, hug someone who needs it, but more than anything, hold on to HOPE...

I believe there is freedom in becoming vulnerable - to recognize and walk through pain - to the joy of life.

With my wishes - and prayers that these pages will help you walk toward love, truth, joy, peace - and into HOPE...

- Debby

There Is Hope for the Struggling

Hope

The silent prayer
hidden in
our hearts
somewhere

'Hope

      God, is hope a silent prayer
      hidden in our hearts somewhere?
    When we believe all hope is gone,
          and there's
              no way
                    we can
                          hold on;
God, is simply remembering You are there,
    and whispering a wordless prayer
    the kind of hope that Jonah tried
        when for
            your grace
                he simply
                    cried?
  God, that's where I am right now -
  tossed and thrown about somehow.
    Lies, like seaweed, strangle me
        and there's
            No hope
              that I
                    can see

God, have I been banished from your sight --
  when I need you most to hold me tight?

    When Jonah felt his life was lost
    he realized there was no cost
      in placing all his hope
        in You.
          Dear God,
            help me
                to do that too!

Your Garden of Hope

If God were to plant you a Garden of Hope,
I know where He would start -
He'd dig into the deepest, blackest soil in your heart.
He'd turn the soil over and sift it through His hands,
and remember how He'd formed you
of special dreams and plans.

He'd pull the weeds of shame and guilt
and the one we call despair.
He'd cry some tears of sorrow over how they'd rooted there.
His tears would wash the memories of failure and of pain,
they'd prepare your heart for planting like a gentle summer rain.

He'd reach into His own heart
to take out a wee, small sprout,
while with His other hand,
He'd scoop aside your patch of doubt.
He'd take that little seed and plant it deep within
a heart that only you could know
had been spoiled by hateful sin.

He'd see the soil of your heart as useful, fertile ground;
the garden He'd plant inside of you
would be like no other one around.
With one small Hope called Jesus planted deep inside,
your heart would grow in faith and love that you could never hide.

If God were to plant you a Garden of Hope,
I know He'd start today,
if you'd simply tell Him of your need
and open up the way.
He'll only come if you ask Him to -
this Gardener of lost souls...
Mercy and Love and Forgiveness
are His only gardening tools

I Wish

Sometimes, I wish God would speak to me,
and explain things I can't always see;
sometimes I wish I wouldn't have to make a choice,
because so loud and clear I'd hear His voice.

Sometimes I'm overcome with doubt and fear
about tomorrow, next week and yet another year;
sometimes I wish I knew just what all lies ahead,
but if I knew, would I wish I didn't know instead?

Sometimes I put my faith through such a test,
because I haven't learned that in His hands there's rest.
Sometimes I want everything done just my way -
and in my time, I want it done today!

Someday, somehow I guess I'll really see
what a wonderful life my God has given me;
if I could only learn to rest in His sweet love
and wait for quiet guidance from above.

Yet I know without hearing one small word
He is now and always will be my one true Lord.
He says, "Don't worry, I have your whole life planned,"
then gently takes a firm hold on my hand.

When God Remains Silent...

When God remains silent, yet for answers I'm yearning,
there must be some lesson that I should be learning.
When I pour out my heart in petitions and pleas,
I know that my eyes cannot see what His sees.
When I think that answers must come in some way,
and it's so hard to simply just trust and obey;
yet God remains silent. Is He really saying,
"My child, now listen; I've heard all your praying.
I see all your tears, and I know your heart's aching.
I know that inside you feel like you are breaking.
I know that you think there is something to do,
but, Child, I am asking just one thing of you.
When I remain silent, please wait patiently.
I'm already doing what you've asked of me.
It's just I know best what needs to be done
to prove my love to each daughter and son."

Blame

Lord, when those men brought that woman to You,
screaming about what she'd done,
were they really trying to cover up
what each of them had become?
Did it somehow make them feel alright
to have those stones to throw?
Did they think if they put all the blame on her
no one would ever know
what each of them was really like -
the secrets they kept inside?
Were those stones they held on to so tightly
the stones of cold, hard pride?
And that man who shouted the loudest -
the one with the steely grey eyes;
did he think the blame he threw at her
would cover up his own lies?
When you knelt to write in the dirt, Lord,
what was it you scribbled there?
Could the men see what You were writing?
Did each see his sin listed there?
By giving them time to accuse, Lord,
and allowing their blame to be clear,
were You really giving each one time
to face up to his biggest fear?
Certainly each one was glad it was she
who was caught in her own ugly sin;
surely they didn't want anyone looking
at what they were deep within.
But, Jesus, I'm glad they brought her to You,
and threw her down at Your feet,
never knowing that what they had done
was cast her before Mercy's seat.
And, Lord, today when we want to throw stones
of hard, cold blame at someone
let those stones remind us instead of
where Blame is coming from.

(based on John 8:1-11; Luke 17:1-4)

Are You?

Are you twisting the truth in the slightest way
    to give it a slant to come out your way ?
Are you taking some words that were said to you
    and repeating them from your own point of view ?
Are you talking about what "So and So" said
    without searching out the facts instead ?
Are you saying that your view's the only right one
    and you can't believe what some other's have done ?
Are you listening fairly to every side -
    taking time to think before you decide ?
Are you looking down deep inside your soul
    and letting the Lord have complete control ?
Are you submissive and yielding to His Holy Light,
    and willing to see there may not be a "right ?"
Are you choosing your cause without hearing all sides,
    or swinging each time the gossip scale slides ?
Are you doing more talking than praying or seeking;
    do you hope to sway God by the way you are speaking ?
Are you thinking that now you'll be justified
    instead of letting God sift out all your pride ?
Are you taking God's matters into your own hands
    and possibly messing up His perfect plans ?
Are you planting words in the right people's ears;
    letting them fight your battle because of their fears ?
Are you manipulating circumstances
    to get the right people to step to your dances ?
Are you asking what lesson you need to be learning,
    or thinking about the points you are earning ?
Are you "being Jesus" in any of this,
    or simply sharing the "Betrayer's Kiss ?"
Are you standing, like Jesus, accused but quiet
    while others around you would cause their riot ?
Are you saying, "Not my will, but God's be done,"
    knowing He'll do what's best for everyone ?
Are you learning to lean on God alone,
    or saying, "I'll take care of this on my own ?"
Are you willing to sit back and rest quietly
    claiming, "God will work all things out for me ?"
Are you able to see His "best" may mean the cross -
    what may be for gain can, at first, look like loss ?
Are you willing to walk this to Calvary,
    to lay it before Him, and just "let it be ?"
Are you ?

Jesus's Tears

As I was praying for you, punctuating with my sighs
all of my frustrations, all my heartaches and my "why's?" -
I pleaded with my Jesus for this whole thing just to end,
hoping that some miracle would change your heart, my friend.
I complained about the lies, how much pain they've caused;
when somewhere in the middle of my praying, as I paused
I turned to look at Jesus, and Friend, it's really true --
Jesus's heart was breaking as He hurt - He cried for you.
I didn't know what I should do, much less - what I should say.
I'd never seen my Jesus break down in quite that way --
so I just sat quietly and listened to His voice.
He explained how His heart aches because you made the choice
to live in such deception, and cultivate your lying
so that lies spill out from you without your even trying.
He said He understands your fear that you might lose someone,
that you might be left alone when all is said and done.
What seems to hurt Him most is how you're so good at deceiving
that many of the lies you've told, you're even now believing!
It seems the devil's made you think your lying is okay,
that all you really have to do is make it right some day -
if you go to church on Sundays, sit quietly and confess,
God will not only excuse you for this, perhaps He'll even bless
your home and life with all that's good. Is that how it appears?
Friend, I'm asking you to look at Jesus's tears.
See? He's crying just for you - He wants to make you whole,
but He can never do that, when deception's in control.
He knows that when you tell the truth life could turn upside down.
When you're willing to take that step, His mercy will be found
in ways you've never dreamed of, through circumstances too -
that all will point to Jesus's most amazing love for you!
Oh, Friend, please look at Jesus' s tears streaming down His face.
Lay down your lies before Him, and trust His warm embrace.

Lord, Help !

Lord, I don't know where I should turn, or what I ought to do...
I only know to come, and bow, and hold this out to You.
I thought this test was over, the trial gone behind -
yet once again it's back to tear my heart and soul and mind!
Oh, God, I'm weak and helpless - with still nothing to show
that I have told the truth and simply want to be let go.
There are so many "Whys?," Lord,
each heart beat shouting one;
Sometimes it seems this whole big mess
will never - ever - be done!
So, God, please look inside me, and see my pain and fear;
then understand the shouts and tears as I am sitting here...
I need Your help to see what ways I ought to move ahead;
I need Your love to fill each place where anger lifts its head.
And, Lord, the fear consumes me
where Your Holy Spirit should -
(it's very terrifying to be so misunderstood)
For those who want to hurt me, Lord, I do not want the same;
please help me control my heart so I won't throw out "Blame."
Your word says You are glorified
when we hold on through the night,
so help my hands cling to You when I fear I'll lose this fight.
Control my every step, Lord, my every word and thought,
so You'll receive the glory when the victory has been bought.
Lord, now I give this all to You - each person that's involved,
every situation until this problem has been solved.
Forgive my doubts and fear, Lord, and fill me with Your peace,
let this become one more way for my faith to increase.
Thank You for this calming time,
though nothing's really changed...
it's just that through this time with You,
my heart's been re-arranged.

Lies

My friend, I feel so sorry for you,
seeing all you put yourself through -
to think you must lie to make someone care,
must be a terrible burden to bear.
Watching every step you take,
careful to never make a mistake
by letting the truth show in some way,
guarding every word that you say
must be tearing you up inside;
do you need someone in whom to confide?
How sad to weave your lies to frame
someone else on whom to blame
your life's problems, struggles, and strife
saying they cause all the pain in your life...
Sometimes I wonder if it's possible now
that you believe your own lies somehow?
Have those lies become your hiding place
from responsibility you might have to face
if you get through the lies to see what's real?
Are you afraid of what you might feel?
I can't imagine what terrible pain
would cause someone to lie to gain
the kind of love that should be received
without another being deceived...
To think you can't be loved as you are -
having to push the lies so far;
to think acting like who you could be
is what your friends would rather see
can only be making you hate yourself more.
My friend, there's one thing of which I'm sure...

God sees through you -yet His love is true..
He'd never turn His back on you -
as long as you're honest before His face,
He'll shower you with mercy and grace.
You could give Him your guilt, fear and shame;
He would trade them for Jesus's name.
He'd wrap you in arms of truth, love and light,
say how you bring Him such delight.
Then He would hold you each step of the way
while you live the truth through every new day.

Handles

If you let go of Anger,
    are you afraid you will fall?
Do all other handles
    seem too small?
Is Forgiveness something
    that you could grasp,
or does that feel
    too great a task?
Is Jealousy burning
    a place in your heart?
Do you need another handle -
    some place to start?
Is your heart gripping
    onto pride
so no one can see
    what is really inside?
Are you clinging to
    some earthly love
instead of looking to
    God up above?
Do you understand
    the need to fear
in order to be able
    to draw near?
Will you hold on to lies
    to cover your shame?
To hide from the truth,
    will you hold onto blame?
To reach out for God,
    you have to let go
of everything else;
    it takes work to say "no."
And saying "yes"
    can be harder still
when it means submitting
    to God's good will.
He's all to hold onto
    when life falls apart.
I know, for I've seen
    how He handles my heart!

Bitterness
rarely hurts
the one
it is directed at,
but can destroy
the one
it is directed from

How Dare You?

How dare you mock my Jesus
and the church that He loves so?
How dare you plan to kill the truth
and then put on a show
of gentleness and humility,
of caring and of good -
raising your hands during singing
like a faithful Christian should?
How dare you plan to hurt someone -
how many? You don't care --
as long as you get what you want,
with power and control both there.
How dare you cheat and lie and plan
to use people as you will?
I have to say of watching you
I've surely had my fill.
I fell for your lies, son of Satan -
I fell for your subtle way;
But now I walk again with God,
and slowly, day by day
my legs are growing stronger,
my feet find solid ground.
I escaped your wicked web.
In God I'm safe and sound.
How dare you say you love Him?
and use His children so?
Haven't you read about Him?
Is it possible you don't know
in spite of it all He loves you?
How can you act, but not feel?
How dare you reject so great a love?
He's waiting for you to get real.

Shame

Lord, I need a heart eraser - one to wipe away the pain...
it isn't that the guilt's there now. It's just this awful shame.
It seemed like such a small thing, trickling in at first.
Now it's overwhelmed me until I feel like I could burst!

Shame's such a heavy blanket wrapped tight around my soul,
how it presses down on me I can't seem to control.
Then, Lord, it keeps reminding me of everything I've done;
instead of feeling free from sin, I feel like Satan's won.

Lord, I know You promised through the blood, in Jesus' name,
that no one who confesses needs to hold on to such shame.
I know You took the guilt from me at such a heavy cost,
because I know and love You, I am no longer lost...

So, Father, when I think of it - what shame is all about:
It's Satan's subtle way to make me feel some fear and doubt
that I could ever please You, or that You really care,
or that my kind of failure is not what You want to bear.

Dear Master, take Your Mercy and move it through me now
to wipe away the shame as I before You humbly bow,
and every place it's held me, Lord, each part it's wrapped around,
write in peace and hope and joy, for I am heaven-bound.

And, Lord, because I know how awful shame can be to bear,
I pray for all the others who need to know You care;
and ask that You would touch them with Your tender Mercy too -
that gentle heart eraser that Your love is poured out through.

Castaways

She has no Daddy's arms for hugs when tears well up inside.
He left to find another's love - he cheated and he lied.
When she comes home after school to an empty, silent place,
she sits down in a darkened room, and stares off in to space.

Another can't express the pain she feels so deep within...
She'd love to talk to anyone - but, where would she begin?
A bottle is her Dad's best friend, her Mom can't settle down;
no time for her, no hope, no love, so she becomes class clown.

Her Daddy's love was twisted; he used her like a toy.
Guilt and shame live in her now, and they've robbed her of all joy.
She hides her hurt in anger, and wishes she could die;
she feels her life is wasted, she keeps on asking, "Why?"

Castaways is what they are - unwanted in their youth;
lonely, hurting, reaching out to find some love and truth.

Their tears don't go
unnoticed.
They're seen by
God above.
His heart breaks, as He reaches out; He knows they need His love.
He'll fill the empty places. He'll share the hurt - the pain.
He'll offer faith and hope and love, as He calls them each by name.

Castaways is what they are; but WANTED in their youth.
Their Father's arms are reaching down to offer love and truth.

Trust

Dear Jesus,
I want to trust You to work things out,
but every day brings some new doubt.
I wonder how long such deception can last.
I long to see it put in the past.
I try to devise a scheme or a plan
that will show the truth about this man;
but there's really nothing I can do
but simply put my trust in You.
If his lying hurts me as much as this -
(and I now understand the betrayer's kiss)
how much his mockery must tear at you
because I know You still love him too!
Help me remember You held on to me
when I was struggling to be free;
help me, Lord, to simply trust
knowing Your ways are always just.
When fear wraps tight around my heart,
and doubt and dread each play their part,
help me remember Whose I am -
a child of the Lion and Lamb.
Help me remember You're holy and true -
to find my sanctuary in You.
For trusting is really resting there -
safe in Your arms of love and care.

*"The Lord is good, a refuge in times of trouble.
He cares for those who trust in him."*
Nahum 1:7

Shepherd

Jesus, I saw you walking away, and I didn't understand.
I thought You'd always be right here, reaching out Your hand...
When I saw Your back toward me, I thought I'd failed You so,
You couldn't forgive me then, and You'd turned away to go.
I knew that I had hurt You, because of what I'd done;
I didn't understand myself - the person I'd become.
I couldn't deal with all the pain I felt so deep within;
instead of turning to You, I thought that I could win
the battles raging in me, without help - on my own.
I didn't know how ugly, Lord, my heart inside had grown.
I'd let my pride and selfishness turn my heart so cold
that Satan and his demons got an icy, chilling hold.
To turn away from your love is not what I had planned.
I'd always felt that when it came to faith in You, I'd stand.
Could that be my biggest mistake - feeling so secure -
I started trusting You less, while my 'faith' I trusted more?
My focus became 'Me,' Lord, instead of only 'You.'
I started thinking about the things You needed "Me" to do.
So that's when I gave in, Lord, to Satan's awful test;
since that moment, Jesus, I haven't found my rest.
But I just looked up again, and though Your back's still turned;
watching how You walk, there is a lesson to be learned.
You haven't turned Your back on me; You haven't turned away;
You haven't stopped Your loving, or listening when I pray!
You've simply said to follow, and what I didn't see
is, as my loving Shepherd, You were gently leading me !

Mercy

I looked in to my Jesus's face
and what I saw was purest grace.
He climbed inside my pain with me,
held me close and just loved me.
I didn't have to say a thing,
yet somehow He knew everything
I felt so far down deep within...
He reached out and took all my sin.
He cupped it in His hand and then
reached toward His heart and put it in
His hand came back with Mercy's light--
He touched my eyes and gave new sight:
Because of who I am inside
with fear and anger - even pride,
sometimes I walk away from Him
and, when I do, I fall to sin.
Still, He doesn't turn away,
refuse to listen when I pray,
or stop His love from pouring down,
or say He'll take away my crown.
He stands with arms held open wide
until I come back to His side
to look into my Jesus's face,
while He looks back in loving grace.

Sunday's Best

I guess we think that it's okay
for us to live our lives each day
doing things we choose to do,
not giving any thought to You
'til Sunday morning comes along...
then - we sing a different song:
We hum a simple hymn or two
while we begin to 'dress' for You.
We pull out humble looks to don
in case somebody's looking on.
Then we put on plastic smiles
concealing secret, sinful styles
of living we've enjoyed all week.
It's Sunday now, we must look meek...
Dear God, we wear an attitude
of such 'church-going' servitude.
while loving looks are well-displayed
to magnify our cool charade.
Oh, Lord, we look so good to me;
for really all that I can see
is what we're wearing - Sunday's best.
It's true, we seem to be so blessed...
But, Lord, You see beyond the pose
of dressing up in Sunday clothes
of prayerful, thoughtful, giving lives.
Lord, you see right through our lies.

You see his hands in prayerful form
conceal a guilty heart that's torn.
Their heads held in defiant pride
hide shame that's buried deep inside;
while laughter fills another's face
who's longing for some touch of grace.
Those tears that cry humility
are really her ability
to mask the anger and the pain
of knowing she'll be hurt again.
Of all the places, Lord, that we
should feel it's safe for us to be
dressed in truth and love and light,
and hold back nothing from Your sight,
Your church is where we ought to go
to wear the Holy Spirit's glow!
Dear God, help us see Sunday's best
is simply when we have confessed
our failings and our needs to You,
and when we're sitting in each pew,
we've not 'put on' a single thing,
but opened naked hearts to sing
in Your own house, beneath Your gaze,
our songs of thanksgiving and praise.
Then, Lord, each day we'll simply rest
knowing we're in Sunday's best.

Church Greetings

As I walked toward church this morning,
I was surprised at my reception
for the greeters standing at the door
were "Anger" and "Deception."
I felt their touch of hatred, saw judgment in their eyes;
and wondered just how long we'd be the target of their lies.
Lord, Satan must be happy to have them in Your place,
for they are such destroyers of Your hope and peace and grace.
They reach out with long tentacles to strangle, or to smother --
not what You planned for how Your church
would act toward one another...
They throw out criticism, or wrap someone in blame,
they cover someone else with guilt, or blanket them with shame.
Their ways are very subtle, they do their work with care --
pretending that they're so concerned, so they need to share
something that they've noticed, or even that they know,
then they sit back and watch their seeds of gossip grow.
Dear God, I'm so frustrated, so tired of the pain
I feel each time I walk toward those church doors once again.
Lord, I don't know what I should do, or even how to pray.
I do know You don't want Your church to be this way.
Dear God, please help me do my part to turn these things around
so as a person comes to church Your mercy is what's found...
Lord, let Your Holy Spirit be the one who guards the door,
so Satan and his demons can have their way no more.
Please fill Your sanctuary with Your glory and Your grace.
Please help each one who comes here to see Jesus face to face.
Lord, fill the halls with angels, and all the classrooms too
and let them do the work that turns
Your people's hearts toward You.
Lord, let the flames of truth and love consume each seeking heart,
Lord, let true forgiveness be the place we find to start.
Lord, fill Your home with laughter - not to hide the pain,
but so each one who enters here finds healing in Your Name.
I love You, Jesus...

Hold on to Hope because God Delights in You!

> "The Lord your God is with you,
> He is mighty to save.
> He will take great delight in you,
> He will quiet you with His love,
> He will rejoice over you with singing."
> Zephaniah 3:17

There Is Hope for the Hurting

Tears
Wordless prayers
that touch
the heart of God...

God's Lap

I climbed onto God's lap to pray
and, as He wiped my tears away,
He looked into my eyes and smiled,
then softly whispered,
"Speak, my child."
I told Him how I hurt inside;
as I did, I cried and cried.
I said I couldn't understand
this kind of testing from His hand,
that it hurt too much to care.
I found the pain too much to bear.
I cried I couldn't take much more,
and wondered if my faith was sure...
I poured out all my questioning
about what good this time could bring.
I even told Him I was mad.
(I thought that would make Him sad)
Then I just broke down and cried;
there were no more words left inside.
I'd gotten all my questions out,
all my frustration, fear and doubt.
He hugged me tight against His chest,
whispered, "Now, it's time to rest."
My sobbing stopped, and then, my sighs;
I rested then, and closed my eyes.
As I did, He hummed a song -
the melody of the twenty-third Psalm.
As He stroked me softly with His hand,
He reminded me that I'm His lamb.

Come, Cry With Me

Have you ever hurt so much inside
that you thought you couldn't cry?
Have you ever raised your fist at God
and screamed an angry, "Why?"
Have you ever been in so much pain
that you couldn't even weep?
Have you ever thought it might hurt less
if you could only sleep?
Have you ever felt your heart
was being torn away from you?
Have you felt the pain of knowing
there was nothing you could do?
Have you wanted to hide in a corner
and wait for another day?
Have you ever felt you didn't
have the energy to pray?
Have you ever felt that life
seems so much harder than it should?
Have you ever longed just simply
not to be misunderstood?

I have hurt so much inside
that I thought I couldn't cry
I have raised my fist at God
and screamed an angry, "Why?"
I have been in so much pain
that I couldn't even weep.
I have thought it might hurt less
if I could only sleep.
I have felt my heart
was being torn in two
I have felt the pain of knowing
there was nothing I could do.

I have wanted to hide in a corner
and wait for another day.
I have felt I didn't
have the energy to pray.
I have felt that life seems
so much harder than it should.
I have longed just simply
not to be misunderstood.

Friend,
if you've felt just one of these,
or maybe even two,
I'd like to reach my hand toward yours
and simply ask you to
"Come, cry with me."
I know this may seem strange,
but I have learned that sharing tears
can often rearrange
the hardest moments in our years,
if we just let them flow;
but sometimes, it takes someone else
to help us let them go.

See, once when I was filled with pain,
and thought my life was through,
a friend reached out her hand toward mine,
and simply asked me to
"Come, cry with me."

And then I did. The tears poured out like rain;
and somehow as the tears flowed out
I couldn't feel the pain
as deeply as I had before -
it had found a sweet release.
Letting go of pain as we shared tears
helped me find some peace...

"Come, cry with me."

For Kyle

A tiny baby, so fragile and new,
gone, before we could say, "We love you."
Those tiny fingers and wisps of hair
would never know your mother's care,
yet somehow, Kyle, we want you to know
how much we love you, even though
you were taken from us, and it tears us apart
that we can only hold you in our broken heart.
See, little one, that's where you grew
before we were sure there would be a "you."
We joined two hearts to make them one
and dreamed of having a fine, little son.
Then, when we heard you were on the way,
we were filled with hope of who you'd be some day.
But, some day is never going to come -
you were taken to heaven before you'd lived one
precious day with your own mom and dad.
You're the beloved child we 'almost' had.
As you're walking with angels through heaven today,
would you please remind them that your mom and dad pray
for the child that they laugh with? - and we can't understand
why God would take you before we'd hold your hand?
Then, maybe they'll say why God needed you there
before we could tell you how much we both care...
And, when you see Jesus, please ask Him to see
how much we love you - your daddy and me?
We're sure He's there, for each day He graces
our lives - in the smiles of your sisters' sweet faces;
we just can't understand why we can't find relief
from this awful feeling of loss - or of grief!
Oh, dear little Kyle, because you're right there,
please tell Him we need the touch of His care
until we arrive in heaven some day
and find you - waiting to show us the way.

Forgiven?

You said you'd forgive me,
but the anger would last -
my mistake was not something
to leave in the past.
I know that I hurt you so much by my sin
that the anger is burning a pain deep within
your own heart, because of what you feel for me.
If you can let go of anger, we might both be free.
I want to be free to hug you again,
to say that I love you, and cry now and then
over God's mercy in both of our lives.
Isn't that the peace for which each of us strives?
When I look in your eyes and see anger and pain,
I remember my failure again and again.
Then I turn to see Jesus, and He calls to me,
"Remember, my blood poured out on Calvary!"
And I do remember - He died for us both.
Learning that is really true growth,
for, my friend, I admit that I have failed you;
but it seems you can't admit you have failed too.
Someday you will see that we all need His grace.
When you do, I hope I'll be in a place
to say that I love you no matter what's past,
and wrap you in arms of love that will last.
For when you've been forgiven, then you can forgive;
it's that touch of God's grace that we all need to live.

Betrayal

Oh, my Dearest Jesus, I really need to see
how You knelt at Judas's feet and washed them tenderly,
knowing he'd betray You, and seeing in his eyes
all the pain that You would feel resulting from his lies.
As You knelt before him, and You looked into his heart,
did it feel as though Your very own was being torn apart?
Did You wish You didn't have to wash his feet,
or share Your bread?
Did You wish that You could tell him
just to go away instead?
Oh, my Dearest Jesus, I really need to feel
the kind of love You had for Judas
as you shared Your meal
with someone who was using You for his own selfish gain.
Dear Jesus, how did You get beyond
the ripping, tearing pain?
How could You still love him
after all You knew he'd done?
How did You ever reach to share
Your cup with such a one?
How did You keep silent so the others wouldn't know
that all his loving acts toward You
were really so much show?
Oh, my Dearest Jesus, help me realize
that sometimes You see Judas
when You look into my eyes;
that if You were to wash my feet,
and share Your cup and bread,
at times in place of love
You'd find the betrayer's kiss instead.
Help me, Dearest Jesus, to kneel down at Your feet
and wash them with my tears
of knowing mercy full and sweet.
And when I share with others
the Communion of Your love,
help me, first, to look inside,
and then to You above.

The Gift of Regret

It amazes me, Lord, how You forget,
while I hold on tightly to regret
over things I've said or something I've done,
when it's all been forgiven by Your precious Son.
Sometimes I wish my memory
could be erased as easily
as a memo board that hangs on a wall -
(would I feel that I'm okay after all?)
I can see the expression on someone's face
when I lashed out with anything but grace;
and I see the pain in another's eyes
when I had no answer for all her "Whys?"
Sometimes it's only my unkind thoughts
that tangle my vine of 'forget-me-nots.'
When I wish, Lord, I could clear my mind
of all those times I've been unkind,
I take a moment to look at You,
and I think I see what You're trying to do...
The memory's not there to cause me pain,
or make me feel regret again.
Instead it's a tool for future days
when someone will need to hear some praise,
or a simple "I'm sorry," or "I understand,"
or, "Here, just hold on tight to my hand."
Regret is a means to wipe away pride -
to help me take a step to the side
so I can see someone else's pain
when they are dealing with failure again.
So, Lord, thank you for the gift of "Regret,"
and help me never to forget
the hard times You have walked me through,
so I can show others the way to You.

Wall of Pain

I'm sitting - staring at this wall
that not so long ago - seemed small;
now, it looms above my head,
weighing me down like heavy lead.
I think back to this wall's creation -
to all that formed its sound foundation -
the angry words, the hurtful looks,
the painful stabs each builder took.
I see some stones I put in place;
in others, I can see your face.
Still, others show some odd reflections
highlighting many imperfections.
At first, I thought my rocks were true
as I stacked them neatly barring you
from seeing how I hurt inside;
(I built the wall so I could hide)
Then, as you added rocks to mine,
it got easier over time
to try to ignore such concrete pain...
Now I try to remember when
it became so hard to see.
I thought the wall protected me.
But, as I sit here all alone
studying each dark, grey stone
I'm seeing what happened in a different light;
now I need you to tell me if I'm right:

It wasn't so much the anger
as all the pain we were going through...
I don't think you knew what to say to me...
I didn't know what to say to you.
But, sometimes, when we hurt so much
we don't know where to turn,
we lash out at the ones we love;
so they hurt us in return.
I hate this wall between us
and want it put away forever;
but I can't do it by myself;
we'll have to work together.
So, here, I'm reaching out my hand -
while I hold on to the hope
you will reach your hand toward mine,
and help me tie a rope
around the wall dividing us,
then help me
        tear
        it
        down;
and everywhere a rock falls,
we'll find some solid ground
to build a bond to hold us -
together - face to face...
then, where once there was a wall
could be a loving place.

My Church

My church is a very hurting place,
have you noticed, just look around...
In every room, or any pew
one who's hurting can be found.
Well, maybe it's not so easy to see -
we all hide it well, you know?
But if you were able to see inside,
you'd see that it is so.
See that lady smiling there -
the one laughing with her friends?
She's afraid to say how badly she hurts,
so she comes here and pretends.
And that man - he's hiding a secret
that's tearing his heart in two,
but you'd never know it to look at him.
He's put on a mask for you.
There, see that little child?
Her heart is breaking inside;
she's been told not to talk about it -
she's learning the lesson of "Pride."
If you could look into the hearts
of anyone who's here,
you'd see some pain or suffering,
some worry or some fear.
Each one who comes is hoping
to find comfort or some rest.
For most, it's a way of coping
to get through a trial or test.
Something's terribly wrong then
when we gather in this place,
if we have to cover up the pain
by pasting a smile on each face.
Wouldn't it be better
if we could let down the guard,
admit we need each other,
that getting through life is hard?

We don't have to give the details
of every little sin.
But knowing I hurt like I do
might give you a place to begin
to talk about your own pain
and what you're going through.
Isn't that what church is really about?
Isn't that what we're to do?
Church should be the safe place
to really be ourselves -
not some plastic, molded mask
we pull from Sunday's shelves.
If I could tell you plainly
how God's forgiven me,
but sometimes that I struggle,
and I don't always feel free,
I wouldn't have to carry
this burden on my own.
Maybe I wouldn't feel like
I have to make it all alone.

Oh, look there in the corner -
do you see those tortured eyes?
Could it be that person needs
to see the truth behind our lies?
If he's to come to Jesus,
to understand His grace,
can he do it in this church?
Can he see it in my face?
Or will he, like so many of us,
begin to 'play the part'
of letting Jesus change his mind,
but holding back his heart?

'Til every one of us agrees
to let our hearts be broken,
all our worship and our praise
is nothing but a token –
an artificial flavoring
we label as "the church."
Is it time we let God inside
to do a thorough search?
Then, as we come together -
them, and you and me,
God could really make this church
all He wants it to be:
a place for those with broken hearts
and true humility,
gentleness and patience
and love that's plain to see.
We'd reach out hearts and hands
to hold each other and to care.
Our burdens would seem lighter,
as we learn it's safe to share.
We'd spend more time in giving,
to find we 'needed' less.
The church that's lived in honesty
is one that God will bless.
I'd like to invite you to my church.
I need you here with me.
If you're a hurting, needy person,
you'll blend in perfectly.
But, please don't put on a mask
or try to look 'just right.'
Each person who comes to my church
is one who needs God's light.

For Now

I want to say something helpful, but I don't know what to say...
I want to be able to tell you that things will be okay...
I want to give you words of hope and bright encouragement too,
but, oh my Precious Friend, none of these are going to do.

I can't understand all the hurts you've walked through up 'til now,
and, even in this time of pain, I know that, still, somehow
you're going to find the strength and faith
to hold on through the tears -
overcoming hopelessness, and moving past your fears.

I've talked to God about you - asked Him why you're tested so,
and even though I've pleaded, I think we'll never know
why someone who's so beautiful - who deserves only what's best -
has so many trials, so little peace and rest...

I told Him I was angry that He allows such pain.
I said you shouldn't have to face such agony again,
I told Him He should help you - yes, I told Him what to do;
then I really think I heard Him say He is holding on to you.

I think I heard Him whisper that He loves you very much,
that He will keep His hand on you, and let you feel His touch.
Then, I thought I felt a tear fall from His eye into my hand;
I think I heard Him say this isn't what He would have planned.

I asked Him then to change things - to make this pain all go away,
I think I heard Him whisper that He will - in Heaven one day..
O Friend, I don't know why you have to go through all this pain -
There are so many things in life we just cannot explain.

Please know the Father loves you.
Don't think you've failed somehow...
This is the only hope I know to offer you for now...

There Is Hope for the Caring

Forgiveness
often brings
more healing
to the one
who gives it,
than to the one
who receives it.

Lord, Let Me Be...

Lord, let me be Your smile
as I go from place to place;
Lord, let me be Your hand
reaching out to offer grace?
Lord, Let me be your shoulder
to the one who needs to cry?
Could I be Your voice reminding them,
"It's alright again to try?"

Lord, I'd like to be Your ears
for the one who needs to talk;
and I'd like to be Your arms
helping someone learn to walk...
Lord, I'd like to be Your heart
to the one whose own is breaking,
and I'd like to be Your hug
for the one whose heart is aching.

Lord, please let me be Your touch
to the one who needs it so,
let me be Your fingers
planting seeds of love to grow?
Lord, let me be these things
for each one You bring my way;
let me show them who You are
in all I do and say?

Lord, one more thing I'd like to ask:
Please let me be Your laughter -
that very special part of You
some don't realize they're after.
Lord, for all these things I ask -
Oh, please just let me be
each and every part of You
that my friends have been for me?

A Rainbow of Love

A Rainbow of Love is in my heart for you;
a rainbow full of dreams and promises too;
it comes from a mixture of laughter and tears,
this rainbow will last throughout all our years.
The shades of blue are for sad times we've shared,
yet through them all we knew each other cared.
The yellows are for all those peaceful times --
to graduations from nursery rhymes.
The purples are treasures we hold deep inside -
wrappings of love that can't be untied.
The reds and oranges are stressful days
that pulled us together in other ways.
Some rainbow colors are brilliant and bright,
while others fade from soft to light,
blending perfectly into each other –
just like we have -- to one another.

Dear Birth Mom

I can't imagine how hard it was for you to make that choice,
knowing you might never see his smile, or hear his voice.
I'm writing you this letter, because I wanted you to know
you made the right decision all those many years ago.
He's grown into a fine young man - the baby that you had;
he knows the choice for you was painful, hard, and sad.
He knows because you loved him, you wanted all life's best,
also that your gift to us has made our lives more blessed.
When you think about him, as I'm sure you often do,
please know that he and we as often thank the Lord for you...
You could have said you didn't want the burden of his life,
a choice to carry him full-term
would cause you too much strife.
You could have said the cost was great,
the pain too much to bear;
but we know you carried him, because of how you care.
More than that, we see your love each day in his eyes --
his sense of humor, tenderness,
and a heart that's sweet and wise.
We think he got these things from you,
and oh, there's so much more;
we know that as he grew in you, you made him very sure
that you cared about him, who he is, who he will be.
What God does with his precious life we're waiting now to see.
So, if you read this letter, know we thank our Lord for you.
We can't imagine any of the pain that you went through
to bring his life into the world, and then kiss him good-bye --
but, if you ever find yourself asking how or why..
just know that he is beautiful - your precious little one,
and he has grown into a handsome, caring, giving son.
He's blessed our lives with so much love,
this child from your heart,
and he has known about you,
and your love from the start.
We often talk about you, we pray that you're okay.
We even often wonder, and hope maybe - someday
we'll wrap our arms around you,
embrace you with our love;
if not while we're still here on earth,
then maybe in heaven above.
So, thank you, Dear Birth Mother, for giving up your child -
through you, our God in heaven looked down on us and smiled.

To Be

God, help me learn what Your word says to do --
to wrap up my whole life in being like You.
Sometimes, I get caught up with all of "the doing,"
and forget it's Your presence I should be pursuing.
Help me to see if I take a step nearer,
Your Word and Your Truth become clearer and dearer.
Help me to see that my schemes and my plans
are not what You want me to place in Your hands.
Help me to take my heart and my soul
and place them completely in Your sweet control.
Help me to see when the testing times come
that I will be closer to You when they're done?
And, Lord, when I ask You for joy and for blessing,
please know that I am really confessing
my faith is simply not yet strong enough
to stay peaceful and calm through times that are tough.
Oh, God, I need You to teach me each day
to give You control of all that I say;
and when I think something must be done by me,
help me remember, I'm only - "to be..."
To be more like Jesus - to show others His grace;
to help them to see how to come face to face
with the One who loves them so much that He died,
and is longing to have them each close by His side.
To be more like Jesus - to care and to share
His love with people everywhere.
Dear God, help me show them what You've asked of me -
it's only like Jesus, You want me - To Be.

Be Like Mom

Mom, When I was little, I'd make quite a mess
going through your closet to find a dress,
then your jewelry and make-up too -
I wanted so much to look like you...
Today, when I think back on those days -
who you are, all your loving ways,
more than ever I know that now,
I still want to look like you somehow.
See, I remember you on your knees
pouring your heart out to God in pleas
for who I would be and what I would do,
Today, I believe He listened to you.
I remember your voice on the telephone
when someone was feeling afraid or alone --
-- how you would let them know you care,
and make them feel like you were right there
standing beside them - holding their hand...
Then I didn't, but now I understand
you gave yourself again and again
to each one in the family, a stranger, or friend.
I'd like to try on your patience today -
it shows in all that you do and you say.
I'd like to be dressed in your kind of love,
for it fits you like some well-worn glove.
And, Mom, if you have some kindness to spare,
it's the kind I need to learn to wear.
Those bracelets of giving you wear on your wrists
would be the next thing on my "Be-like-Mom" list.
I'd like to walk in your tenderness too,
for you wear it like a comfortable shoe.
Then, I'd wrap a coat of grace about me
wanting it to be easy for people to see
that it's knit together - a special blending -
of love and forgiveness that's never-ending.
I guess I could stay in your room all day
trying on those things you give away
without ever thinking about yourself.
Would you tuck this someplace up on a shelf,
to look at it every now and then?
And know that I still like to pretend
that someday, Mom, I'll be just like you -
that's the best thing I could ever do!

My Grandma's Hands

If I close my eyes I still can see my Grandma's hands,
and although she's up in heaven, I hope she understands
how much she meant to me-how much I learned there at her side
as I watched those little fingers that spread so far and wide.
My Grandma's hands were busy from the very break of day,
when she'd get up with a smile, and send Grand Pap on his way
to the fields to do some plowing, or picking what had grown.
While he got busy with his chores, she started on her own...
She'd milk the cow and put her out to pasture, rain or sun,
then she'd collect the chicken's eggs,
and when those things were done,
she'd cook a great big breakfast, and have it waiting there
ready for my Grand Pap - right by his favorite chair.
She had to pump the water into the big old kitchen sink
and fill some pots to heat up on the old wood stove... I think
she always did these things with a smile on her face;
I still can hear her humming songs of God's *"Amazing Grace."*
Depending on what day it was, there was laundry to be done
in big old kettles outside, over fires, in the sun.
On some days we'd make butter, taking all the cream
that she'd skimmed off old Guernsey's milk.
To me it always seemed
she liked to crank the handle, she made it feel like play,
as she'd throw in a little salt, and tell her story of the day.
Of, course we all got to help - each begging for a turn
to crank the handle for her as we'd hear the butter churn.
The best days were those mornings
we knew she'd be baking bread -
she'd be up and started before we jumped out of bed.
She'd have the wood stove heated up with just a log or two,
and as we each would wander in, she'd give us jobs to do:
"Now, sift the flour, there - that's good."
"Could you run to get a little more wood ?"
"Your turn to knead it, punch it down!"
"You can't bake bread if you're wearing a frown! "
We'd knead and work to make it right
knowing there would be a fight
over who got the crust - but Grandma was able
to cut all crust pieces to fill up her table.

Sometimes we'd sit out on the swing,
and Grandma would ask us all to sing
an old church hymn or a Sunday School song;
but it never seemed so very long
before there was much more work to do
and she really needed our help too.
When her hands showed me how to milk the cow
and I couldn't hit the bucket, somehow
instead of getting upset with me
she just kept trying patiently
to show me how it should be done.
She always made everything seem like fun.
Planting a garden was a special delight;
or catching small piglets on a summer's night
when they'd escaped their pen again,
would lead her to a "Remember when..."
Then we'd hear stories -- I think all true
of things she'd learned, or things she knew.
With flour on her apron, and hands on her hips
she'd fill our minds with quotes and quips
that I wish I could remember today,
but I never thought she'd go away...
She would tuck us into her mother's bed
on cold winter nights, there was no heat; instead
she'd warm up bricks in the old wood stove
and I remember how I always dove
deep down in the covers to stretch my feet
toward the bricks she'd wrapped and put under the sheet.
Oh, the sound on the farm that I loved best
were those nights when I laid down to rest
as the gentle rain on the tin roof fell...
Why is it I remember so well
those days we spent near my Grandma's hands?
I guess some part of me now understands
those days, long past, are a part of me -
that place we cherish as memory?
More than that - down deep within
is a longing I cannot begin
to explain. Beyond the shadow of any doubt
I'll see those hands and hear her shout.
When I step in to eternity
My Grandma's hands will be hugging me.

This Jar of Clay

Lord, fill this simple Jar of Clay
with words of Truth from You each day;
help me see that when I pray,
You tune Your ear to all I say?
Lord, help me stand with others too,
to share the joy we know in You,
then show me how to be and do
each thing that You would ask me to?
Pour Yourself out into me,
(though plain and simple I may be)
fill me so each one can see
Your treasure for eternity!

A Friend Just Like You

If God granted wishes like He answers prayer,
and I thought He had a 'wish answer' to spare...
I'd ask Him to make a friend just like you
for everybody - My Dear Friend, it's true!
Each person on earth would have someone who's caring,
in good times and hard times, a friend who'd be sharing
all of the laughter - then all of the tears,
a hug for their joys, and a heart for their fears ...
A person who'd know the dark secrets inside -
who would still call them 'friend,' and smile with pride.
Each person on earth would have someone to see
success out of failure like you've done for me.
They'd see how one could forgive and forget,
and learn to let go of their shame and regret.
They'd always have someone to listen and pray,
to assure them that things will be better one day.
Each person would have someone
who's always extending
unconditional love that just has no ending...

If God granted wishes - My Dear Friend, it's true!
Every person on earth would have someone like you!

Shadow

Lord, help me rest beneath the shadow of Your hand;
not worry so much about things I have planned ?
Help me, Lord, to trust You with each detail of my life -
while I strive to be a Godly mother, faithful friend, and wife?
Lord, when there are circumstances I cannot control,
help me see that You allow some things to make me whole:
that if each day were filled with comfort, peace and joy,
life would just reflect some simple, mindless wind-up toy.
Help me look at hard times as waiting, learning places
so I can lean on Your strong arm no matter what life faces.
Teach me to thank You, Father, for tests and trials too
where I can know there's nothing for me but to trust in You.
Help me look toward heaven when life has pulled me down,
find my peace and comfort in knowing You're around.
God, help me reflect Jesus in my heart and in my smile,
and share His love with those I meet - even for a while.
Please, God, hold on to me when my faith is growing weak;
sift each word through Your kind heart every time I speak?
Fill me with your hope, Lord, and let it overflow
to every one I meet - in every place I might go.
Yes, Father, always keep me in that shadow of Your hand
so everyone I meet, Lord, can see and understand
that You are all I long for - my safe and hiding place -
the shadow is Your ever-present mercy, love and grace.
Thank You, God, for loving me, as only You could do,
and asking me to snuggle, right up close to You.

The Gift I Call "You"

Let's pretend I just knelt - down on one knee
and found a beautiful package that's labeled "for Me."
I admire the present - wrapped with such care,
and wonder who could have put it right there.
As carefully as I know how to do,
I begin to unwrap the Gift I call "You."
I look at the ribbon, and peek 'neath the bow,
to see beautiful eyes with a warm, loving glow -
eyes that sparkle like the sun on the sea,
that dance when they're laughing, or looking at me.
Then I slowly unfold the wrap side to side
to find the wonderful treasure hidden inside!
Tucked in a corner of giving and grace,
I look at my very own Mother's face!
There's strength in this layer, humility too,
wrapped up in hands that love what they do.
A Grandmother's heart is tucked deep inside
with just the right touch of 'Grand-motherly pride.'
Tucked under some tissue I've just noticed here
is courage to help wipe away some dear friend's tear.
Encouragement's wrapped in a layer of care,
and wisdom's woven through angel hair.
This gift is filled through every part
with My Most Beautiful 'Mother's Heart.'
I look through the box of your self-less giving,
and think of each moment that I have been living:
I know from the moment my life was conceived
that deep down inside you, I've always believed
God was designing His best gift for me.
You're this beautiful package - the one that I see...
I love you.

There Is Hope for the Searching

My Most Common Prayer:
Lord, Help!

His Most Comforting Answer:
Trust Me.

From Memories to Dreams

We're standing at this point in time
facing two directions:
ahead to images and dreams;
back memory's reflections.
A memory is a treasure,
something we hold dear,
of what has gone on in the past
but think of through the years.
It takes us back to other times,
youthful fun-filled days
of special people, places, things
that touched us on our ways.
That memory lingers in our hearts
and slumbers there unheeded,
but gentle nudging wakes it so
it comes to mind when needed.
What keeps us going - moving on
are all our hopes and dreams
of things we want to do and see --
accepting all life deems!
A dream's a vision showing us
so much that can be done -
of lives to touch and steps to take,
unique for every one.
These dreams help mold a person's goals
and give him some direction.
but looking forward always makes us
glance back in reflection.
For God's design entwines the two
with His invisible seams,
giving purpose through each life
From Memories to Dreams.

A Priceless Treasure

A priceless treasure? Lord, is that what You see
when You look at this filthy rag I call, "Me?" --
this rag that is soiled by such guilt and shame,
that so often finds itself soaking up pain?

A priceless treasure? Lord, please look again
at what this rag is holding within --
a rag stained with so many failures and faults --
it couldn't be destined for Your treasured vaults!

A priceless treasure? Lord, open my eyes
and help me to look past all of the lies
that the enemy places for me to soak in,
so that all I can see is the stains of my sin...

A priceless treasure? This rag that shines bright
because Jesus's blood has turned it to white?
Lord, help me remember what You've done for me,
and that I'm Your treasure for eternity!

Like a Child

Oh, Jesus, I see You standing there!
I guess You heard my simple prayer...
now You want me to walk to You?
Do You know that's a scary thing to do?
Yes, I see Your smiling face.
I feel the warmth of Your loving grace,
I see Your arms reaching out for me,
and I know Your love is truly free.
But, Jesus, I'm so afraid I'll fall;
I really don't trust myself at all.
My legs and feet don't want to move,
and I don't think others would approve
of how I'm being drawn to You.
See, Jesus, they all know me too-
they know my temper and my pride;
they've each seen my ugly side...
"It doesn't matter what they think," You say?
"I'm put together in just the right way?"
"You like me exactly as I am?"
"You formed me with Your very own hand?"
"You want me to move a little closer now?"
But, Jesus, I really don't know how!
"One small step is all I need take?"
But, Jesus, I don't want to make a mistake!
Alright, I'll keep my eyes on You
and I'll do whatever You tell me to.
"Just walk into Your warm embrace?"
Oh, Jesus, I think I've found my place!"

(based on Matthew 18:3,4)

So I Can Praise You

"Let me live so I can praise You."
was a prayer from David's heart.
Dear Lord, please let those words
become the most important part
of my every waking moment,
my every thought and deed - -
"To live a life of praise to You,"
I very humbly plead.

The next verse says he wandered
like a sheep who'd gone astray,
and Lord, You know my mind
and heart so often go that way.
Please, Father, hold on to me,
keep Your hand in mine,
reminding me that You
are right here with me all the time.

Let every word I speak, Lord,
and every thing I do
be offered as a sacrifice of praise,
Dear God, to You.!
Let every breath I take, Lord,
be wrapped in Your embrace
so everyone I ever touch
will be blessed by Your grace.

(based on Psalm 119:175-176)

I've Been Held in His Arms

When I get to heaven I'll realize
I've been held in His arms all along.
When I close my eyes here, and open them there
to join in that heavenly song --
I'll see that each time I felt heartache or pain,
or acknowledged I'd failed Him in some way again,
I'd never fallen too far from His grace;
but instead, He has held me in His warm embrace.
When I get to heaven - it's then that I'll see
so clearly, just how much my Jesus loves me!

Forever Friends

Would you be one of my Forever Friends -
be with me in Heaven, where life never ends?
We'll walk in the Light of Mercy and Grace
and gaze on God's holy, precious face!
We'll dance with angels on feathered wings
and walk with Jesus whose praises rings
throughout all of eternity!
Dear Friend, will you be there in Heaven with me?
Would you be one of my Forever Friends -
live with me in heaven where Love never ends;
where fear and doubt, heartache and pain
will never - ever be felt again?!
Where so many friends and family
will be there? Yes! Eternally!
See, death can't knock on heaven's door -
It's going to be banished forevermore!
Would you be one of my Forever Friends -
see past our today's to where Time never ends?
Where cities are filled with God's Goodness and Light -
and there's never a need to go through some dark night...
Where Laughter and Song fill each moment - each prayer -
and God's praises are heard every day - every where.
There, Peace will be found on each person's face -
There just won't be room for pain in that Place!
Could you be one of my Forever Friends? -
one walking in Truth - who never pretends
that life is easy down here on earth;
and sometimes you wonder what makes it all worth
living? Struggling? Day to day?
When people are hurting, do you know what to say?
Ask them to be your Forever Friends,
tell them of Heaven where life never ends...
Offer them Hope - in Jesus's Name
and assure them life will not be the same
when they give Him all their worry and care
Because He's in Heaven - waiting there
Looking for His Forever Friends,
and building a Kingdom where Life never ends.
Do you think we could be Forever Friends?

Heaven

Lord, I'm standing in a multitude
before Your heavenly throne,
yet I feel as though I'm basking in Your presence, all alone.
As I join with all the others to sing praises to Your name
I cannot help but wonder if each one here feels the same...

I've waited, oh so long, Lord,
to see You face to face -
to tell you how I thank You for Your amazing grace;
for all Your tender mercies, Your love and goodness too;
the reason that I'm standing here is very simply - You.

Yet, Father, as I look around
this vast and peopled sea,
it seems as though Your gaze is focused, Lord, right here - on me!
Oh God, of all these people, who could have failed You more,
who could have feared and doubted, or been more insecure?

But You don't seem to notice
as You look into my eyes
and reach Your hand to offer me another sweet surprise -
it is a crown of glory - a victor's crown so bright
it splashes rainbow colors upon my robe of white!

And then, my dear, sweet Jesus,
You hug me to Your chest,
and I am overwhelmed, Lord, by how much You have blessed
first, my life on earth, by walking with me there
and now by offering heaven - so very free of care.

I fall prostrate before You,
and kiss Your wounded feet,
and lay my crown before You as You sit in mercy's seat.
Then, Lord, I join with angels and every other soul
to sing Your heavenly praises, for You have made me whole.

Remember...

If you're remembering me today,
please take some time to think and pray..
for where I am is heavenly,
and soon, you could be here with me...
singing songs of thanks and praise
to God for all His loving ways;
kneeling here to say a prayer
for all His love and tender care.
I'm not alone. There is a crowd
who sing with me, and say out loud
they're glad to be here in this place -
to gaze upon our Savior's face.
We never walk alone, in fear;
I haven't seen a single tear!
or heard a little baby's cry,
or had the time to stop and sigh.
Here, children have a special place -
their playground's near the throne of Grace.
He walks with them, holds their hands,
tells them that He still has plans
for all that Heaven's going to be
someday when you're all here with me...
I know how you may miss me there,
but please, know that I have no care
except to see you walk with Him...
for that's where this must all begin.

When I was there so close to you,
deep inside your heart you knew
that I drew close to God each day,
and longed for you to live that way.
That's why I'm with my Father now,
and hope that you can see somehow
life on earth's a flickering flame -
what really matter's is Jesus's Name
always present on our lips;
His grace flowing from our fingertips...
Then maybe, not too far away,
you'll join me here to laugh and play,
singing songs with heaven's crowds
and dance - with angels through the clouds!

Dear Friends and Precious Family,
each time you remember me -
hold on to Hope - through God above -
and wrap yourself up in His love...
Remember, I'm in Heaven today -
the slightest, gentlest breath away;
with no more heartache; no more pain
and if you love Jesus, you'll see me again!

Remember...

The Cup and the Bread

When I take Communion,
Dear Jesus, help me see
everything You are;
who You want me to be.
Help me, Lord, to look ahead
to that very special day
when I'll sit at Heaven's table,
and I'll get to hear You say,
"Welcome home, My child,
please share My cup and bread;
I've made a place here for you
just as I had said."

(based on Matthew 26:27-29)

Home

Once upon a time - which could mean "today,"
    a man went to heaven and heard Jesus say,
    "Welcome home, Child, I've been waiting for you,
    and so has each one who has come before you!"
    He looked around at the crowd that was cheering
    his presence there, and then - through a clearing,
the man glimpsed a mansion of glorious height.
    Jesus said, "Son, it's yours!" with a smile of delight.
    Out of the crowd walked his mother and dad;
    as they hugged him warmly, they said they were glad
    to see him at last, and welcomed him "home,"
    as tears filled his eyes at the joy in their own...
Then Jesus said, "Let's take a walk
    through heaven now, and have a talk
    about eternity here in this place."
    The man loved the smile on Jesus's face.
    Each one in the crowd stepped back as they passed,
    welcoming him, "You've made it at last!"
They walked on streets that were paved with gold,
    just as John's revelation foretold.
    It seemed within seconds, they were at the door
    of the home that would be his forever more.
    Jesus smiled and said, "For a job well done,
    made just for you - our precious one."
Jesus handed the man a simple key.
    He said, "Open the door now, look and see
    all that We put here - designed just for you --
    because you were always faithful to do
    what Our Father had said you should.
    We know that you always meant to do good."
For the first time since he'd arrived in this place,
    the man saw the smile leave Jesus's face,
    and he wondered what had caused it to leave;
    but he turned toward his door - he just couldn't believe
    the beauty of his heavenly home;
    Jesus smiled again - and said, "Child, it's your own!"
The key opened the door and the man stepped inside,
    and looked at a staircase - one high, deep and wide...
    "It represents our great love for you,"
    Jesus said to the man, "because you tried to be true."
    Once again, the man saw the smile
    leave Jesus' face for a little while...

Each room in the mansion was amazing to see.
    "Jesus, are you sure it's for me?"
    Jesus nodded and said, "Let's walk for a while."
    The man watched His face and wished for the smile.
    Then, when they stepped outside his door,
    the man looked around and grew unsure...
He glanced to his left, and then to his right
    and saw other mansions glorious and bright.
    Each one's owner was standing there
    waving at him, and offering to share
    their hearts and homes and lives with him.
    He grabbed Jesus's arm, started trembling within.
"Jesus! What are you doing to me?
    You can't make me spend eternity
    with all of these people! They don't belong here!
    You know on earth I made it clear
    that those kind of people would have no place
    in heaven, Lord! Just look at his face!"
Jesus looked at the man he was pointing to,
    and smiled, "Oh, I love him. I really do!"
    Then the man turned his face toward another's eyes
    and his voice cried out his anguished surprise,
    "Lord, you can't expect me to live next door
    to a woman who was once a whore."
"Oh, I do," Jesus said with a grin,
    "My blood has washed away her sin,
    just as clearly as it washed yours,
    she belongs here - on heaven's shores!"
    One by one, as he looked around,
    the man discovered that he'd be bound
for all of time to live with those
    whom on earth he had closed
    his heart and mind to. He'd decided there
    they weren't the kind Jesus wanted to share
    His life and love with, so the man had chosen
    to shut them out. His heart became frozen.
Every home around his, the man could see
    was occupied for eternity
    by someone he had judged on earth
    as coming up short. Not one was worth
    the blood Jesus shed upon the cross...
    Then, seeing the man was at a loss

for words to express what he was feeling,
> Jesus said, "My friend, it's time for healing..."
> The man said, "But, Lord, I don't understand...
> I mean... this can't be what You planned -
> to make me live every day - next to them?!"
> "But that's exactly the plan, my dear friend,"

Jesus said, with a tender look on His face
> filled with compassion and flowing with grace.
> The man began listing each thing he had done
> while he was on earth - for Jesus, God's Son;
> Who stood there listening, then once in a while,
> nodded or shook His head with a smile.

When the man stopped his listing, he said, "Jesus, You see,
> these are the reasons that You should love me;
> but look at those people - they're different for sure,
> and I really don't want them living next door."
> Jesus looked and suggested, "Child, look again -
> each one you're judging is My personal friend."

No, they didn't do much good, like you've said,
> but they each have done something better instead."
> Jesus invited him to walk by His side
> introducing him with warm, glowing pride.
> As he met all his neighbors, the man's heart was broken,
> and it was some time before his thoughts could be spoken...

"Oh, Jesus, I'm sorry! Please, Lord forgive me?
> There's so much I know now that I didn't see!
> Each person I've met - every one in this place
> has reached out to someone in Your loving grace!
> My list of good works is nothing but pride.
> What matters is having Your love inside!"

Jesus pressed His pierced palm gently on the man's chest,
> said he was healed, so now he could rest...
> What that man learned as they both had walked -
> as he met each person, and watched as they talked
> was how each one had let Jesus's heart in.
> The outside didn't matter - what did was within.

Once upon a time, which could mean today --
> will you open your heart, and push pride away?
> Could you make room for Jesus to fill every place
> where you would show judgement instead of God's grace?
> If you do my friend, there's just no pretending,
> this story will have a
> > Happy Ending!

NOTES